Where did they hide my presents ?

To Emma, a silly dilly
thrilling editor and friend
—A. K.

To DJ, my kid who wears
painty pants too
—D. C.

ISBN-13: 978-0-439-93311-7
ISBN-10: 0-439-93311-0

Text copyright © 2005 by Alan Katz. Illustrations copyright © 2005 by David Catrow. All rights reserved. Published by Scholastic Inc., 557 Broadway, New York, NY 10012, by arrangement with Margaret K. McElderry Books, an imprint of Simon & Schuster Children's Publishing Division. SCHOLASTIC and associated logos are trademarks and/or registered trademarks of Scholastic Inc.

12 11 10 9 8 7 6 5 4 3 2
6 7 8 9 10 11/0

Printed in the U.S.A.   40

First Scholastic printing, December 2006

Book design by Sonia Chaghatzbanian

The text of this book is set in Kosmik.

The illustrations are rendered in watercolors, colored pencil, and ink.

Where did they hide my presents?

silly dilly Christmas songs

Alan Katz and David Catrow

SCHOLASTIC INC.
New York   Toronto   London   Auckland   Sydney
Mexico City   New Delhi   Hong Kong   Buenos Aires

Santa Claus Is All Over Town

(To the tune of "Santa Claus Is Coming to Town")

Oh, he's happy and grand
He's jolly and stout
I can't understand
How he dashes about
Santa Claus is all over town!

I stop at the bank
He's there—ho, ho, ho!
Then always shows up
The next place that I go
Santa Claus is all over town!

I see him at the market
I see him on the street
He doesn't go by reindeer
Must have turbo-powered feet!

That speedy Saint Nick
Is hard to believe
He zips round so quick,
Training for Christmas Eve
Santa Claus is all over town!

The Sugarplum Fairy

(To the tune of "The Little Drummer Boy")

Dance, they told me
I'm the Sugarplum
A Nutcracker fairy
And I feel so dumb
I hope I don't fall down
And land on my bum
Right now I wish I were as
Small as Tom Thumb
Small as a crumb
I feel so glum.

What an audience
Where did they come from?
They're clapping wildly
I'm thrilled and I'm numb
A great experience
This thing has become
It's really fun to dance
I'm the Sugarplum
Sugarplum yum
Sugarplum yum!

Two more shows this week
I'm the Sugarplum
Hope that you'll come!

Our Friendly Mailman

(To the tune of "Frosty the Snowman")

Our friendly mailman
Has a big bag on his back
With a billion cards and some packages
Twice the size of Santa's sack!

Our friendly mailman
Works in ice and sleet and snow
He comes without fail
To bring us the mail
Got no time to ho, ho, ho!

He doesn't have a reindeer sleigh
To help when things get tough
If it were me, I'd probably
Just stay home and keep the stuff!

But our friendly mailman
Brings a lot of gifts each day
When the mail slot clanks,
I peek out, say "Thanks"
Then our mailman's on his way!

Toy Catalogs

(To the tune of "O Tannenbaum")

Toy catalogs
Toy catalogs
Each morning I inspect 'em
They're volumes of
The stuff I love
That's why I must collect 'em
These days they're truly all I read
They're crammed with stuff I truly need
I take care of
Toy catalogs
I guard and I protect them.

I'm copying
My catalogs
So Santa will know better
I've circled everything I want
'Cause I don't need a sweater
A building set, a bass guitar
A jumbo jet, a racing car
Dear Santa Claus, I'm sorry it's
A thirty-nine-page letter.

Toy catalogs
Toy catalogs
They make me so ecstatic
But thanks to these
Toy catalogs,
My life is problematic
If Santa brings each thing I ask,
To fit it all will be a task
My room is filled with catalogs,
So I'll move to the attic!

Pick Me Up!

(To the tune of "Sleigh Ride")

We're at our town's tree lighting,
A place exciting to be
But with adults so tall
There is nothing at all I can see.

The stores have fancy windows,
So women and men go with glee
No matter how I beg,
The back of their legs is
All I see!

Pick me up! Pick me up! Pick me up! Let's go!
Lemme look at the show
I'm missing the whole thing, don't you know?
Pick me up! Pick me up! Pick me up! Be swift!
It would be a gift
Instead of a stroller, next time
Bring me in a forklift!

The crowds are never stopping,
And all the shopping is rushed
Remember I am tiny
Don't let my hiney get crushed!

Although I love the season,
When you're small, there's a reason to fear
Let's go watch Christmas specials
And stay in the house till next year!

At the Malls

(To the tune of "Deck the Halls")

At the malls
No parking spaces
Ma Ma Ma Ma Ma
Can't we go home?

Million cars
Ten parking places
Ma Ma Ma Ma Ma
Can't we go home?

You said this would be a fun day
Ma Ma Ma
Ma Ma Ma
Let's go home
This could take till Easter Sunday
Ma Ma Ma Ma Ma
Can't we go home?

All this circling is a dumb thing
Ma Ma Ma Ma Ma
Can't we go home?
There we can make Grandma something
Ma Ma Ma Ma Ma
Can't we go home?

What's that, Mom? You're shopping for me?
Ma Ma Ma
Ma Ma Ma
Please let's stay
Let's keep looking, it won't bore me
Who cares if we drive
Around all day!

Snowball Fight

(To the tune of "Jingle Bells")

Dashing through the house
'Cause I can't find my left boot
Gotta head outside
This one'll be a beaut
The powder's two feet deep
Whole front lawn is white
We'll stomp and we'll attack,
And we won't come back till midnight. Oh . . .

Snowball fight
Snowball fight
Join us if you dare
We'll make sure a clump of snow
Lands in your underwear!

Snowball fight
Snowball fight
Favorite winter sport
We'll pelt until it melts,
And we will never leave our fort!

Johnny can't come out
'Cause he's stuck inside with flu
He's a snowball champ,
So here is what we do
With buckets full of snow
We step up to his door
We ring his bell
He answers it
We start a snowball war! Oh . . .

Snowball fight
Snowball fight
Snow flies left and right
Johnny's living room
Is now all covered up in white.

Snowball fight
Snowball fight
Gee, our moms are sore
We may not get outside
Till at least the next spring thaw!

Where Did They Hide My Presents?

(To the tune of "Rudolph the Red-Nosed Reindeer")

I checked cupboards, the attic, the basement, the closets
When it comes to world's best gift hiding, my mom's it
Not one box in sight
So to me, it's not a good night!

Where did they hide my presents?
That is what I'd like to know
Searching all night's not pleasant
I looked high and low and low.

I even checked the freezer
No toys, just some pumpkin pie
My dad is such a teaser
Someone call the FBI!

Hey, I think I see a box
Underneath the couch
Can't tell what it is, it's wrapped
Oh no, here comes Mom—I'm trapped!

I will lie still and silent
Hope she'll turn around and leave
Might be stuck with the package
Under here till Christmas eve!

Something in My Brother's Underpants

(To the tune of "Winter Wonderland")

Doorbell rings
Gee, who is it?
Party guests
Christmas visit
The mood is so swell
But what is that smell?
Something in my brother's underpants!

Now I don't
Like complaining
But my dad's
Entertaining
The guests and my mom
Don't smell the stink bomb
Something in my brother's underpants!

From the basement we can hear the laughter
Parents sharing cheer while eggnog flows
Christmas songs are ringing from the rafter
How can I sing along
And hold my nose?

Upstairs it's super-duper
This kid's a party pooper
Mom, please don't deck the halls
Come change his overalls
There's something in my brother's underpants!

Twim the Twee

(To the tune of "Let It Snow")

It's the moment we've all been waiting
Yes, it's time for decorating
Baby sister, Sue, squeals with glee
Twim the twee, twim the twee, twim the twee!

Grab the ornaments, let's unpack 'em
And please don't let sister crack 'em
Gotta handle this carefully
Twim the twee, twim the twee, twim the twee!

Hanging balls, bells, and popcorn strands
It's a job for big folks, not for Sue
Two-year-olds have such tiny hands
There's nothing babies can do.

As we stand back to admire,
Sue hangs up her pacifier
It completes the job beautifully
Twim the twee, twim the twee, twim the twee!

We're Caroling

(To the tune of "O Christmas Tree")

We're caroling
We're caroling
We're singing of the season
Eyes full of tears
Can't feel my ears
It's way, way below freezin'!

I mostly cough
Instead of hum
Some toes snapped off
My lips are numb
The coldest day in history
My singing's filled with
Sneezin'.

We're caroling
We're caroling
What do we do this stunt for?
I'm wearing fourteen sweaters and
Three hats I had to hunt for.

I do not mean to be a pain,
But it's so cold
I'll freeze my brain
My mom says, "Please do not complain.
We haven't left our front door!"

Hanging Lights

(To the tune of "Silent Night")

Hanging lights
Not flashing bright
Bulbs don't work
It's not right
I hold ladders as Daddy climbs
He's been on the roof four hundred times
Dad refuses to lose
Just blew another fuse!

Hanging lights
What a fight
Nothing glows
Dark all night
Dad's checked millions of bulbs for a goof
He's eating all his meals up on the roof
We don't know what to think
Twinkling lights just won't twink.

Hanging lights
Fail to excite
Each bulb dim
Sad, sad sight
Mom says maybe it's time to come down
Neighbors are laughing at Dad throughout town
Dad's up there night and day
It's now the middle of May.

There Are Lots of Things I Will Warn 'Bout Christmas

(To the tune of "It's Beginning to Look a Lot Like Christmas")

My advice is don't stand beneath that doorway
It's got mistletoe
Someone near you just might insist
You allow yourself to be kissed
If you don't look out above, look out below!

Also, careful 'cause they are serving eggnog
Just what's in that stuff?
It is gloppy and thick like paste
And one teeny, tiny taste
And you've had enough!

There is something else I will warn 'bout Christmas
Candy cane alert
Though they're hanging from every tree,
Don't go eating eighty-three
They're yummy, but your tummy's gonna hurt!

So to all of you, I wish Merry Christmas
Here's a final scoop
After Santa comes with his sleigh,
Just remember the next day:
Watch for reindeer poop!

Batteries

(To the tune of "Silver Bells")

Christmas morning
Dad is yawning
'Cause he wrapped gifts all night
There are toys piled high to the ceiling
Robots can't talk
Dollies won't walk
All because Dad forgot
The one thing that we need millions of . . .

Batteries
Batteries
All of our gifts aren't working
Cs and Ds
Father, please
Get hundreds of triple-As!

In his pj's
Dad says "Okay,"
And he heads to the car
For the things that will get our toys humming
Daddy's sneezing
'Cause it's freezing,
And as he turns the key,
Nothing happens and we hear Dad moan . . .

"Battery
Battery
The one in this car needs replacing
I am stuck
A tow truck
Is what I'll get Christmas day!"